THE

Sylphs of the Seasons,

WITH

OTHER POEMS.

BY

W. ALLSTON.

LONDON:

PRINTED FOR W. POPLE, 67, CHANCERY LANE.

1813.

CONTENTS.

THE

SYLPHS OF THE SEASONS;

A POET'S DREAM.

Prefatory Note

TO THE

SYLPHS OF THE SEASONS.

As it may be objected to the following Poem, that some of the images there introduced are not wholly peculiar to the Season described, the Author begs leave to state, that, both in their selection and disposition, he was guided by that, which, in his limited experience, was found to be the Season of their greatest impression: and, though he has not always felt the necessity of pointing out the collateral causes by which the effect was increased, he yet flatters himself that, in general, they are sufficiently implied either by what follows or precedes them. Thus, for instance, the *running brook*, though by no means peculiar, is appropriated to Spring; as affording by its motion and *seeming* exultation one of the most lively images of that spirit of renovation which animates the earth after its temporary suspension during the Winter. By the same rule, is assigned to Summer the *placid lake*, &c. not because that image is never seen, or enjoyed, at any other season; but on account of its affecting us more in Summer, than either in the Spring, or in Autumn; the indolence and languor generally then experienced disposing us to dwell with particular delight on such an object of repose, not to mention the grateful idea of coolness derived from a knowledge of its temperature. Thus also the *evening cloud*, exhibiting a fleeting representation of successive objects, is, perhaps, justly appropriated to Autumn, as in that Season the general decay of inanimate nature leads the mind to turn upon itself, and without effort to apply almost every image of sense or vision of the imagination, to its own transitory state.

If the above be admitted, it is needless to add more; if it be not, it would be useless.

THE

SYLPHS OF THE SEASONS.

LONG has it been my fate to hear
The slave of Mammon, with a sneer,
My indolence reprove.
Ah, little knows he of the care,
The toil, the hardship that I bear,
While lolling in my elbow-chair,
And seeming scarce to move :

For, mounted on the Poet's steed,
I *there* my ceaseless journey speed
O'er mountain, wood, and stream :
And oft within a little day
'Mid comets fierce 'tis mine to stray,
And wander o'er the Milky-way
To catch a Poet's dream.

But would the Man of Lucre know
What riches from my labours flow ?—
A DREAM is my reply.
And who for wealth has ever pin'd,
That had a World within his mind,
Where every treasure he may find,
And joys that never die !

One night, my task diurnal done,
(For I had travell'd with the Sun
    O'er burning sands, o'er snows)
Fatigued, I sought the couch of rest;
My wonted pray'r to Heaven address'd;
But scarce had I my pillow press'd
    When thus a vision rose.

Methought within a desert cave,
Cold, dark, and solemn as the grave,
    I suddenly awoke.
It seem'd of sable Night the cell,
Where, save when from the ceiling fell
An oozing drop, her silent spell
    No sound had ever broke.

There motionless I stood alone,
Like some strange monument of stone
Upon a barren wild;
Or like, (so solid and profound
The darkness seem'd that wall'd me round)
A man that's buried under ground,
Where pyramids are pil'd.

Thus fix'd, a dreadful hour I past,
And now I heard, as from a blast,
A voice pronounce my name:
Nor long upon my ear it dwelt,
When round me 'gan the air to melt,
And motion once again I felt
Quick circling o'er my frame.

Again it call'd; and then a ray,
That seem'd a gushing fount of day,
    Across the cavern stream'd.
Half struck with terror and delight,
I hail'd the little blessed light,
And follow'd 'till my aching sight
    An orb of darkness seem'd.

Nor long I felt the blinding pain;
For soon upon a mountain plain
    I gaz'd with wonder new.
There high a castle rear'd its head;
And far below a region spread,
Where every Season seem'd to shed
    Its own peculiar hue.

Now at the castle's massy gate,
Like one that's blindly urged by fate,
A bugle-horn I blew.
The mountain-plain it shook around,
The vales return'd a hollow sound,
And, moving with a sigh profound,
The portals open flew.

Then ent'ring, from a glittering hall
I heard a voice seraphic call,
That bade me " ever reign,
" All hail!" it said in accent wild,
" For thou art Nature's chosen child,
" Whom wealth nor blood has e'er defil'd,
" Hail, Lord of this Domain!"

And now I paced a bright saloon,
That seem'd illumin'd by the moon,
So mellow was the light.
The walls with jetty darkness teem'd,
While down them chrystal columns stream'd,
And each a mountain torrent seem'd,
High-flashing through the night.

Rear'd in the midst, a double throne,
Like burnish'd cloud of evening shone;
While, group'd the base around,
Four Damsels stood of Faery race;
Who, turning each with heavenly grace
Upon me her immortal face,
Transfix'd me to the ground.

And *thus* the foremost of the train:
Be thine the throne, and thine to reign
O'er all the varying year!
But ere thou rulest the Fates command,
That of our chosen rival band
A Sylph shall win thy heart and hand,
Thy sovereignty to share.

For we, the sisters of a birth,
Do rule by turns the subject earth
To serve ungrateful man;
But since our varied toils impart
No joy to his capricious heart,
'Tis now ordain'd that human art
Shall rectify the plan.

Then spake the Sylph of Spring serene,
'Tis *I* thy joyous heart I ween,
    With sympathy shall move :
For I with living melody
Of birds in choral symphony,
First wak'd thy soul to poesy,
    To piety and love.

When thou, at call of vernal breeze,
And beck'ning bough of budding trees,
    Hast left thy sullen fire ;
And stretch'd thee in some mossy dell,
And heard the browsing wether's bell,
Blythe echoes rousing from their cell
    To swell the tinkling quire :

Or heard from branch of flow'ring thorn
The song of friendly cuckoo warn
    The tardy-moving swain;
Hast bid the purple swallow hail;
And seen him now through ether sail,
Now sweeping downward o'er the vale,
    And skimming now the plain;

Then, catching with a sudden glance
The bright and silver-clear expanse
    Of some broad river's stream,
Beheld the boats adown it glide,
And motion wind again the tide,
Where, chain'd in ice by Winter's pride,
    Late roll'd the heavy team:

Or, lur'd by some fresh-scented gale,
That woo'd the moored fisher's sail
    To tempt the mighty main,
Hast watch'd the dim receding shore,
Now faintly seen the ocean o'er,
Like hanging cloud, and now no more
    To bound the sapphire plain;

Then, wrapt in night the scudding bark,
(That seem'd, self-pois'd amid the dark,
    Through upper air to leap,)
Beheld, from thy most fearful height,
Beneath the dolphin's azure light
Cleave, like a living meteor bright,
    The darkness of the deep:

'Twas mine the warm, awak'ning hand
That made thy grateful heart expand,
And feel the high control
Of Him, the mighty Power, that moves
Amid the waters and the groves,
And through his vast creation proves
His omnipresent soul.

Or, brooding o'er some forest rill,
Fring'd with the early daffodil,
And quiv'ring maiden-hair,
When thou hast mark'd the dusky bed,
With leaves and water-rust o'erspread,
That seem'd an amber light to shed
On all was shadow'd there ;

And thence, as by its murmur call'd,
The current traced to where it brawl'd
    Beneath the noontide ray;
And there beheld the checquer'd shade
Of waves, in many a sinuous braid,
That o'er the sunny channel play'd,
    With motion ever gay:

'Twas I to these the magick gave,
That made thy heart, a willing slave,
    To gentle Nature bend;
And taught thee how with tree and flower,
And whispering gale, and dropping shower,
In converse sweet to pass the hour,
    As with an early friend:

That mid the noontide sunny haze
Did in thy languid bosom raise
    The raptures of the boy;
When, wak'd as if to second birth,
Thy soul through every pore look'd forth,
And gaz'd upon the beauteous Earth
    With myriad eyes of joy:

That made thy heart, like HIS above,
To flow with universal love
    For every living thing.
And, oh! if I, with ray divine,
Thus tempering, did thy soul refine,
Then let thy gentle heart be mine,
    And bless the Sylph of Spring.

And next the Sylph of Summer fair ;
The while her crisped, golden hair
Half veil'd her sunny eyes :
Nor less may *I* thy homage claim,
At touch of whose exhaling flame
The fog of Spring that chill'd thy frame
In genial vapour flies.

Oft by the heat of noon opprest,
With flowing hair and open vest,
Thy footsteps have I won
To mossy couch of welling grot,
Where thou hast bless'd thy happy lot,
That thou in that delicious spot
May'st see, not feel, the sun :

Thence tracing from the body's change,
In curious philosophic range,
The motion of the mind;
And how from thought to thought it flew,
Stillh oping in each vision new
The faery land of bliss to view,
But ne'er that land to find.

And then, as grew thy languid mood,
To some embow'ring silent wood
I led thy careless way;
Where high from tree to tree in air
Thou saw'st the spider swing her snare,
So bright!—as if, entangled there,
The sun had left a ray:

Or lur'd thee to some beetling steep
To mark the deep and quiet sleep
That wrapt the tarn below ;
And mountain blue and forest green
Inverted on its plane serene,
Dim gleaming through the filmy sheen
That glaz'd the painted show ;

Perchance, to mark the fisher's skiff
Swift from beneath some shadowy cliff
Dart, like a gust of wind ;
And, as she skimm'd the sunny lake,
In many a playful wreath her wake
Far-trailing, like a silvery snake,
With sinuous length behind.

Nor less when hill and dale and heath
Still Evening wrapt in mimic death,
Thy spirit true I prov'd:
Around thee, as the darkness stole,
Before thy wild, creative soul
I bade each faery vision roll,
Thine infancy had lov'd.

Then o'er the silent sleeping land,
Thy fancy, like a magick wand,
Forth call'd the Elfin race:
And now around the fountain's brim
In circling dance they gaily skim;
And now upon its surface swim,
And water-spiders chase;

Each circumstance of sight or sound
Peopling the vacant air around
    With visionary life :
For if amid a thicket stirr'd,
Or flitting bat, or wakeful bird,
Then straight thy eager fancy heard
    The din of Faery strife ;

Now, in the passing beetle's hum
The Elfin army's goblin drum
    To pigmy battle sound ;
And now, where dripping dew-drops plash
On waving grass, their bucklers clash,
And now their quivering lances flash,
    Wide-dealing death around :

———

Or if the moon's effulgent form
The passing clouds of sudden storm
In quick succession veil;
Vast serpents now, their shadows glide,
And, coursing now the mountain's side,
A band of giants huge, they stride
O'er hill, and wood, and dale.

And still on many a service rare
Could I descant, if need there were,
My firmer claim to bind.
But rest I most my high pretence
On that my genial influence,
Which made the body's indolence
The vigour of the mind.

And now, in accents deep and low,
Like voice of fondly-cherish'd woe,
The Sylph of Autumn sad:
Though I may not of raptures sing,
That grac'd the gentle song of Spring,
Like Summer, playful pleasures bring,
Thy youthful heart to glad;

Yet still may I in hope aspire
Thy heart to touch with chaster fire,
And purifying love:
For I with vision high and holy,
And spell of quick'ning melancholy,
Thy soul from sublunary folly
First rais'd to worlds above.

What though be mine the treasures fair
Of purple grape and yellow pear,
　　And fruits of various hue,
And harvests rich of golden grain,
That dance in waves along the plain
To merry song of reaping swain,
　　Beneath the welkin blue;

With these I may not urge my suit,
Of Summer's patient toil the fruit,
　　For mortal purpose given:
Nor may it fit my sober mood
To sing of sweetly murmuring flood,
Or dies of many-colour'd wood,
　　That mock the bow of heaven.

But, know, 'twas mine the secret power
That wak'd thee at the midnight hour,
In bleak November's reign :
'Twas I the spell around thee cast,
When thou didst hear the hollow blast
In murmurs tell of pleasures past,
That ne'er would come again :

And led thee, when the storm was o'er,
To hear the sullen ocean roar,
By dreadful calm opprest;
Which still, though not a breeze was there,
Its mountain-billows heav'd in air,
As if a living thing it were,
That strove in vain for rest.

'Twas I, when thou, subdued by woe,
Didst watch the leaves descending slow,
To each a moral gave;
And as they mov'd in mournful train,
With rustling sound, along the plain,
Taught them to sing a seraph's strain
Of peace within the grave.

And then uprais'd thy streaming eye,
I met thee in the western sky
In pomp of evening cloud;
That, while with varying form it roll'd,
Some wizard's castle seem'd of gold,
And now a crimson'd knight of old,
Or king in purple proud.

And last, as sunk the setting sun,
And Evening with her shadows dun,
  The gorgeous pageant past,
'Twas then of life a mimic shew,
Of human grandeur here below,
Which thus beneath the fatal blow
  Of Death must fall at last.

Oh, then with what aspiring gaze
Didst thou thy tranced vision raise
  To yonder orbs on high,
And think how wondrous, how sublime
'Twere upwards to their spheres to climb,
And live, beyond the reach of Time,
  Child of Eternity!

And last the Sylph of Winter spake;
The while her piercing voice did shake
    The castle-vaults below.
Oh, youth, if thou, with soul refin'd,
Hast felt the triumph pure of mind,
And learnt a secret joy to find
    In deepest scenes of woe;

If e'er with fearful ear at eve
Hast heard the wailing tempest grieve
    Through chink of shatter'd wall;
The while it conjur'd o'er thy brain
Of wandering ghosts a mournful train,
That low in fitful sobs complain,
    Of Death's untimely call:

Or feeling, as the storm increas'd,
The love of terror nerve thy breast,
    Didst venture to the coast;
To see the mighty war-ship leap
From wave to wave upon the deep,
Like chamoise goat from steep to steep,
    'Till low in valleys lost;

Then, glancing to the angry sky,
Behold the clouds with fury fly
    The lurid moon athwart;
Like armies huge in battle, throng,
And pour in vollying ranks along,
While piping winds in martial song
    To rushing war exhort:

Oh, then to me thy heart be given,
To me, ordain'd by Him in heaven
    Thy nobler powers to wake.
And oh! if thou with poet's soul,
High brooding o'er the frozen pole,
Hast felt beneath my stern control
    The desert region quake;

Or from old Hecla's cloudy height,
When o'er the dismal, half-year's night
    He pours his sulph'rous breath,
Hast known my petrifying wind
Wild ocean's curling billows bind,
Like bending sheaves by harvest hind,
    Erect in icy-death;

Or heard adown the mountain's steep
The northern blast with furious sweep
Some cliff dissever'd dash;
And seen it spring with dreadful bound
From rock to rock, to gulph profound,
While echoes fierce from caves resound
The never-ending crash:

If thus, with terror's mighty spell
Thy soul inspir'd, was wont to swell,
Thy heaving frame expand;
Oh, then to me thy heart incline;
For know, the wondrous charm was mine
That fear and joy did thus combine
In magick union bland.

Nor think confin'd my native sphere
To horrors gaunt, or ghastly fear,
    Or desolation wild:
For I of pleasures fair could sing,
That steal from life its sharpest sting,
And man have made around it cling,
    Like mother to her child.

When thou, beneath the clear blue sky,
So calm no cloud was seen to fly,
    Hast gaz'd on snowy plain,
Where Nature slept so pure and sweet,
She seem'd a corse in winding-sheet,
Whose happy soul had gone to meet
    The blest Angèlic train;

Or mark'd the sun's declining ray
In thousand varying colours play
    O'er ice-incrusted heath,
In gleams of orange now, and green,
And now in red and azure sheen,
Like hues on dying dolphins seen,
    Most lovely when in death;

Or seen at dawn of eastern light
The frosty toil of Fays by night
    On pane of casement clear,
Where bright the mimic glaciers shine,
And Alps, with many a mountain pine,
And armed knights from Palestine
    In winding march appear:

'Twas I on each enchanting scene
The charm bestow'd that banish'd spleen
Thy bosom pure and light.
But still a *nobler* power I claim ;
That power allied to poets' fame,
Which language vain has dar'd to name—
The soul's creative might.

Though Autumn grave, and Summer fair,
And joyous Spring demand a share
Of Fancy's hallow'd power,
Yet these I hold of humbler kind,
To grosser means of earth confin'd,
Through mortal *sense* to reach the mind,
By mountain, stream, or flower.

But mine, of purer nature still,
Is *that* which to thy secret will
    Did minister unseen,
Unfelt, unheard; when every sense
Did sleep in drowsy indolence,
And Silence deep and Night intense
    Enshrowded every scene;

That o'er thy teeming brain did raise
The spirits of departed days*
    Through all the varying year;
And images of things remote,
And sounds that long had ceas'd to float,
With every hue, and every note,
    As living now they were:

---

* In a late beautiful poem by Mr. Montgomery is the following line: "*The spirits of departed hours.*" The Author, fearing that so singular a coincidence of thought and

And taught thee from the motley mass
Each harmonizing part to class,
(Like Nature's self employ'd;)
And then, as work'd thy wayward will,
From these with rare combining skill,
With new-created worlds to fill
Of space the mighty void.

Oh then to me thy heart incline;
To me whose plastick powers combine
The harvest of the mind;
To me, whose magic coffers bear
The spoils of all the toiling year,
That still in mental vision wear
A lustre more refin'd.

---

language might subject him to the charge of plagiarism, thinks it necessary to state that his poem was written long before he had the pleasure of reading Mr. M.'s.

She ceas'd—And now in doubtful mood,
All motionless and mute I stood,
Like one by charm opprest:
By turns from each to each I rov'd,
And each by turns again I lov'd;
For ages ne'er could one have prov'd
More lovely than the rest.

"Oh blessed band, of birth divine,
What mortal task is like to mine!"—
And further had I spoke,
When, lo! there pour'd a flood of light
So fiercely on my aching sight,
I fell beneath the vision bright,
And with the pain I woke.

THE TWO PAINTERS:

A TALE.

THE

TWO PAINTERS:

A TALE.

SAY why in every work of man
Some imperfection mars the plan?
Why join'd in every human art
A perfect and imperfect part?
Is it that life for art is short?
Or is it nature's cruel sport?
Or would she thus a moral teach;
That man should see, but never reach,
The height of excellence, and show
The vanity of works below?
Or consequence of Pride, or Sloth;
Or rather the effect of both?

Whoe'er on life his eye has cast,
I fear, alas, will say the last!

Once on a time in Charon's wherry
Two Painters met, on Styx's ferry.
Good sir, said one, with bow profound,
I joy to meet thee under ground,
And though with zealous spite we strove
To blast each other's fame above,
Yet here, as neither bay nor laurel
Can tempt us to prolong our quarrel,
I hope the hand which I extend
Will meet the welcome of a friend.
Sweet sir! replied the other Shade,
While scorn on either nostril play'd,
Thy proffer'd love were great and kind
Could I in thee a *rival* find.—
A rival, sir! return'd the first,
Ready with rising wind to burst,

Thy meekness, sure, in this I see;
We are not rivals, I agree:
And therefore am I more inclin'd
To cherish one of humble mind,
Who apprehends that one above him
Can never condescend to love him.

Nor longer did their courteous guile,
Like serpent, twisting through a smile,
Each other sting in civil phrase,
And poison with envenom'd praise;
For now the fiend of anger rose,
Distending each death-wither'd nose,
And, rolling fierce each glassy eye,
Like owlets' at the noonday sky,
Such flaming vollies pour'd of ire
As set old Charon's phlegm on fire.
Peace! peace! the grizly boatman cried,
You drown the roar of Styx's tide;

Unmanner'd ghosts! if such your strife,
'Twere better you were still in life!
If passions such as these you show
You'll make another Earth below;
Which, sure, would be a viler birth,
Than if we made a Hell on Earth.
At which in loud defensive strain
'Gan speak the angry Shades again.
I'll hear no more, cried he; 'no more'
In echoes hoarse return'd the shore.
To Minos' court you soon shall hie,
(Chief Justice here) 'tis he will try
Your jealous cause, and prove at once
That only dunce can hate a dunce.

Thus check'd, in sullen mood they sped,
Nor more on either side was said;
Nor aught the dismal silence broke,
Save only when the boatman's stroke,

Deep-whizzing through the wave was heard,
And now and then a spectre-bird,
Low-cow'ring, with a hungry scream,
For spectre-fishes in the stream.

Now midway pass'd, the creaking oar
Is heard upon the fronting shore;
Where thronging round in many a band,
The curious ghosts beset the strand.
Now suddenly the boat they 'spy,
Like gull diminish'd in the sky;
And now, like cloud of dusky white,
Slow sailing o'er the deep of night,
The sheeted group within the bark
Is seen amid the billows dark.
Anon the keel with grating sound
They hear upon the pebbly ground,
And now with kind, officious hand,
They help the ghostly crew to land.

What news? they cried with one accor
I pray you, said a noble lord,
Tell me if in the world above
I still retain the people's love:
Or whether they, like us below,
The motives of a Patriot know?
And me inform, another said,
What think they of a Buck that's dead?
Have they discern'd that, being dull,
I knock'd my wit from watchmen's skull?
And me, cried one, of knotty front,
With many a scar of pride upon 't,
Resolve me if the world opine
Philosophers are still divine;
That having hearts for friends too small,
Or rather having none at all,
Profess'd to love, with saving grace,
The *abstract* of the human race?

And I, exclaim'd a fourth, would ask
What think they of the Critick's task ?
Perceive they now our shallow arts ;
That merely from the want of parts
To write ourselves, we gravely taught
How books by others should be wrought ?
Whom interrupting, then inquir'd
A fifth, in squalid garb attir'd,
Do now the world with much regard
In mem'ry hold the dirty Bard,
Who credit gain'd for genius rare
By shabby coat and uncomb'd hair ?
Or do they, said a Shade of prose,
With many a pimple's ghost on nose,
Th' eccentric author still admire,
Who wanting that same genius' fire,
Diving in cellars underground,
In pipe the spark ethereal found :
Which, fann'd by many a ribbald joke,
From brother tipplers puff'd in smoke,

Such blaze diffused with crackling loud,
As blinded all the staring croud?
And last, with jealous glancing eye,
That seem'd in all around to pry,
A Painter's ghost in voice suppres'd,
Thus questioning, the group address'd;

Sweet strangers, may I too demand,
How thrive the offspring of my hand?
Whether, as when in life I flourish'd,
They still by puffs of fame are nourish'd?
Or whether have the world discern'd
The tricks by which my fame was earn'd;
That, lacking in my pencil skill,
I made my tongue its office fill:
That, marking (as for love of truth)
In others' works a limb uncouth,
Or face too young, or face too old,
Or colour hot, or colour cold;

Or hinting, (if to praise betray'd)
'Though colour'd well, it yet might *fade*;'
And 'though its grace I can't deny,
Yet pity 'tis so hard and dry.'—
I thus by implication show'd
That mine were wrought in better mode;
And talking thus superiors down,
Obliquely raise my own renown?
In short, I simply this would ask,—
If Truth has stript me of the mask;
And, chasing Fashion's mist away,
Expos'd me to the eye of day——
* A Painter false, without a heart,
Who lov'd himself, and not his art?

* The Author would be sorry to have it supposed that he alludes here to any individual; for he can say with truth, that such a character has never fallen under his observation: much less would he be thought to reflect on the Artists, as a class of men to which such baseness may be generally imputed. The case here is merely *supposed*, to

At which, with fix'd and fishy gaze,
The Strangers both express'd amaze.

---

shew how easily imbecility and selfishness may pervert this most innocent of all arts to the vilest purposes. He may be allowed also to disclaim an opinion too generally prevalent; namely, that envy and detraction are the natural offspring of the art. That Artists should possess a portion of these vices, in common with Poets, Musicians, and other candidates for fame, is reasonably to be expected; but that they should exclusively monopolise them, or even hold an undue proportion, 'twere ungenerous to suppose. The Author has known Artists in various countries; and can truly say, that, with a very few exceptions, he has found them candid and liberal; prompt to discover merit, and just in applauding it. If there have been exceptions, he has also generally been able to trace their cause to the unpropitious coincidence of narrow circumstances, a defective education, and poverty of intellect. Is it then surprising, that in the hands of such a triumvirate the art should be degraded to an imposture, to the trick of a juggler? but it surely would be a cause of wonder, if, with such leprous members, the sound and respectable body of its professors should escape the suspicion of partaking their contamination.

Good Sir, said they, 'tis strange you dare
Such meanness of yourself declare.

Were I on earth, replied the Shade,
I never had the truth betray'd;
For there (and I suspect like you)
I ne'er had time myself to view.
Yet, knowing that 'bove all creation
I held myself in estimation,
I deem'd that what I *lov'd* the *best*
Of every virtue was possess'd.
But *here* in colours black and true,
Men see themselves, who never knew
Their motives in the worldly strife,
Or real characters through life.
And here, alas! I scarce had been
A little day, when every sin
That slumber'd in my living breast,
By Minos rous'd from torpid rest,

Like thousand adders, rushing out,
Entwin'd my shuddering limbs about.—
Oh, strangers, hear!—the truth I tell—
That fearful sight I saw was Hell.
And, oh! with what unmeasur'd wo
Did bitterness upon me flow,
When thund'ring through the hissing air,
I heard the sentence of Despair—
'Now never hope from Hell to flee;
Yourself is all the Hell you see!'—

He ceas'd. But still with stubborn pride
The Rival Shades each other eyed;
When, bursting with terrifick sound,
The voice of Minos shook the ground,
The startled ghosts on either side,
Like clouds before the wind, divide;
And leaving far a passage free,
Each, conning his defensive plea,

With many a crafty lure for grace,
The Painters onward hold their pace.
Anon before the Judgement Seat,
With sneer confronting sneer they meet:
And now in deep and awful strain,
Piercing like fiery darts the brain,
Thus Minos spake. Though I am he,
From whom no secret thought may flee;
Who sees it ere the birth be known
To him, that claims it for his own;
Yet would I still with patience hear
What each may for himself declare,
That all in your defence may see
The justice pure of my decree.—
But, hold!—It ill beseems my place
To hear debate in such a case:
Be therefore thou, Da Vinci's shade,
Who when on earth to men display'd

The scatter'd powers of human kind
In thy capacious soul combin'd;
Be thou the umpire of the strife,
And judge as thou wert still in life.

Thus bid, with grave becoming air,
Th' appointed judge assum'd the chair.
And now with modest-seeming air,
The rivals straight for speech prepare:
And thus, with hand upon his breast,
The Senior Ghost the Judge address'd:
The world, (if ought the world I durst
In this believe) did call me first
Of those, who by the magick play
Of harmonizing colours, sway
The gazer's sense with such surprise,
As make him disbelieve his eyes.
'Tis true that some of vision dim,
Or squeamish taste, or pedant whim,

My works assail'd with narrow spite;
And, passing o'er my colour bright,
Reproach'd me for my want of grace,
And silks and velvets out of place;
And vulgar form, and lame design,
And want of character; in fine,
For lack of worth of every kind
To charm or to enlarge the mind.
Now this, my Lord, as will appear,
Was nothing less than malice sheer,
To stab me, like assassins dark,
Because I did not hit a mark,
At which (as I have hope of fame)
I never once design'd to aim:
For seeing that the life of man
Was scarcely longer than a span;
And, knowing that the Graphic Art
Ne'er mortal master'd but *in part*;

I wisely deem'd 'twere labour vain,
Should I attempt the *whole* to gain;
And therefore, with ambition high,
Aspir'd to reach what pleas'd the eye;
Which, truly, sir, must be confess'd,
A part that far excels the rest:
For if, as all the world agree,
'Twixt Painting and fair Poesy
The diff'rence in the mode be found,
Of colour this, and that of sound,
'Tis plain, o'er every other grace,
That colour holds the highest place;
As being that distinctive part,
Which bounds it from another art.
If therefore, with reproof severe
I've galled my pigmy Rival here,
'Twas only, as your Lordship knows,
Because his foolish envy chose

To rank his classic forms of mud
Above my wholesome flesh and blood.

Thus ended parle the Senior Shade.
And now, as scorning to upbraid,
With curving, *parabolick* smile,
Contemptuous, eying him the while,
His Rival thus: 'Twere vain, my Lord,
To wound a gnat by spear or sword*;
If therefore *I*, of greater might,
Would meet this *thing* in equal fight,
'Twere fit that I in size should be
As mean, diminutive, as he;
Of course, disdaining to reply,
I pass the wretch unheeded by.

---

* "Who breaks a butterfly upon a wheel?"

Pope.

But since your Lordship deigns to know
What I in my behalf may show,
With due submission, I proclaim,
That few on earth have borne a name
More envied or esteem'd than mine,
For grace, expression, and design,
For manners true of every clime,
And composition's art sublime.
In academick lore profound,
I boldly took that lofty ground,
Which, as it rais'd me near the sky,
Was thence for vulgar eyes too high ;
Or, if beheld, to them appear'd
By clouds of gloomy darkness blear'd.
Yet still that misty height I chose,
For well I knew the world had those,
Whose sight, by learning clear'd of rheum,
Could pierce with ease the thickest gloom,

Thus, perch'd sublime, 'mid clouds I wrought,
Nor heeded what the vulgar thought.
What, though with clamour coarse and rude
They jested on my colours crude;
Comparing with malicious grin,
My drapery to bronze and tin,
My flesh to brick and earthen ware,
And wire of various kinds my hair;
Or (if a landscape-bit they saw)
My trees to pitchforks crown'd with straw;
My clouds to pewter plates of thin edge,
And fields to dish of eggs and spinage;
Yet this, and many a grosser rub,
Like fam'd Diogenes in tub,
I bore with philosophic nerve,
Nay, gladly bore; for, here observe,
'Twas that which gave to them offense,
Did constitute my excellence.—

I see, my Lord, at this you stare :
Yet thus I'll prove it to a hair.—
As Mind and Body are distinct,
Though long in social union link'd,
And as the only power they boast,
Is merely at each other's cost ;
If both should hold an equal station,
They'd both be kings without a nation :
If therefore, one would paint the Mind
In partnership with Body join'd,
And give to each an equal place,
With each an equal truth and grace,
'Tis clear the picture could not fail
To be without or head or tail.
And therefore as the Mind alone
I chose should fill my graphick throne,
To fix her pow'r beyond dispute,
I trampled Body under foot :

That is, in more prosaick dress,
As I the passions would express,
And as they ne'er could be portray'd
Without the subject Body's aid,
I show'd no more of that than merely
Sufficed to represent them clearly:
As thus—by simple means and pure
Of light and shadow, and contour:
But since what mortals call complexion,
Has with the mind no more connexion
Than ethicks with a country dance,
I left my col'ring all to chance;
Which oft (as I may proudly state)
With Nature war'd at such a rate,
As left no mortal hue or stain
Of base, corrupting flesh, to chain
The Soul to Earth; but, free as light,
E'en let her soar till out of sight.

Thus spake the champion bold of mind;
And thus the Colourist rejoin'd:
In truth, my Lord, I apprehend,
If I by *words* with him contend,
My case is gone; for he, by gift
Of what is call'd the *gab*, can shift
The right for wrong, with such a sleight,
That right seems wrong and wrong the right;
Nay, by his twisting logick make
A square the form of circle take.
I therefore, with submission meet,
In justice do your Grace intreat
To let awhile your judgment pause,
That *works* not *words* may plead our cause.
Let Merc'ry then to Earth repair,
The works of both survey with care,
And hither bring the best of each,
And save us further waste of speech.

Such fair demand, the Judge replied,
Could not with justice be denied.
Good Merc'ry, hence ! I fly, my Lord,
The Courier said. And, at the word,
High-bounding, wings his airy flight
So swift his form eludes the sight ;
Nor aught is seen his course to mark,
Save when athwart the region dark
His brazen helm is spied afar,
Bright-trailing like a falling star.

And now for minutes ten there stole
A silence deep o'er every soul—
When, lo ! again before them stands
The courier's self with empty hands.
Why, how is this ? exclaim'd the twain ;
Where are the *pictures*, sir ? Explain !
Good sirs, replied the God of Post,
I scarce had reach'd the other coast,

When Charon told me, one he ferried
Inform'd him they were dead and buried:
Then bade me hither haste and say,
Their ghosts were now upon the way.
In mute amaze the Painters stood.
But soon upon the Stygian flood,
Behold! the spectre-pictures float,
Like rafts behind the towing boat:
Now reach'd the shore, in close array,
Like armies drill'd in Homer's day,
When marching on to meet the foe,
By bucklers hid from top to toe,
They move along the dusky fields,
A grizly troop of painted shields:
And now, arrived in order fair,
A gallery huge they hang in air.

The ghostly croud with gay surprize
Began to rub their stony eyes:

Such pleasant lounge, they all averr'd,
None saw since he had been interr'd;
And thus, like connoisseurs on Earth,
Began to weigh the pictures' worth:
But first (as deem'd of higher kind)
Examin'd they the works of *Mind.*
* Pray what is this? demanded one.—
That, sir, is Phœbus, alias, Sun:
A classick work you can't deny;
The car and horses in the sky,
The clouds on which they hold their way,
Proclaim him all the God of Day.—

---

* The Author having no revenge to gratify, and consequently no pleasure in giving pain, has purposely excluded the Works of all living Artists from this Gallery.

Nay, learned sir, his dirty plight
More fit beseems the God of Night.
Besides, I cannot well divine
How mud like this can ever shine.—
Then look at that a little higher.—
I see 'tis Orpheus, by his lyre.
The beasts that listening stand around,
Do well declare the force of sound:
But why the fiction thus reverse,
And make the power of song a curse?
The ancient Orpheus soften'd rocks,
Yours changes living things to blocks.—
Well, this you'll sure acknowledge fine,
Parnassus' top with all the Nine.
Ah, *there* is beauty, soul and fire,
And all that human wit inspire!—
Good sir, you're right; for being stone,
They're each to blunted wits a hone.—

And what is that? inquir'd another.—
That, sir, is Cupid and his Mother.—
What, Venus? sure it cannot be:
That skin begrim'd ne'er felt the sea;
That Cupid too ne'er knew the sky;
For lead, I'm sure, could never fly.—
I'll hear no more, the Painter said,
Your souls are, like your bodies, dead!

With secret triumph now elate,
His grinning Rival 'gan to prate.
Oh, fie! my friends; upon my word,
You're too severe: he should be *heard;*
For *Mind* can ne'er to glory reach,
Without the usual aid of *speech.*
If thus howe'er, you seal his doom,
What hope have I unknown to Rome?
But since the *truth* be your dominion,
I beg to hear your just opinion.

This picture then—which some have thought
By far the best I ever wrought—
Observe it well with critick ken;
'Tis Daniel in the Lion's Den.—
'Tis flesh itself! exclaim'd a Critick.
But why make Daniel paralytick?
His limbs and features are distorted,
And then his legs are badly sorted.
'Tis true, a miracle you've hit,
But not as told in Holy Writ;
For there the miracle was braving,
With *bones unbroke*, the Lion's craving;
But yours (what ne'er could man befall)
That he should *live with none at all.*—
And pray, inquir'd another spectre,
What Mufti's that at pious lecture?
That's Socrates, condemn'd to die;
He next, in sable, standing by,

Is Galen*, come to save his friend,
If possible, from such an end;
The other figures, group'd around,
His Scholars, wrapt in woe profound.—
And am I like to this portray'd?
Exclaim'd the Sage's smiling Shade.
Good Sir, I never knew before
That I a Turkish turban wore,
Or mantle hemm'd with golden stitches,
Much less a pair of satin breeches;
But as for him in sable clad,
Though wond'rous kind, 'twas rather mad
To visit one like me forlorn,
So long before himself was born.—

---

* To those who are conversant with the Works of the Old Masters this piece of anachronism will hardly appear exaggerated.

And what's the next ? inquir'd a third ;
A jolly blade upon my word !—
'Tis Alexander, Philip's son,
Lamenting o'er his battles won ;
That now his mighty toils are o'er,
The world has nought to conquer more.
At which, forth stalking from the host,
Before them stood the Hero's Ghost.—
Was that, said he, my earthly form,
The Genius of the battle-storm ?
From top to toe the figure's Dutch !
Alas, my friend, had I been such,
Had I that fat and meaty skull,
Those bloated cheeks, and eyes so dull,
That driv'ling mouth, and bottle nose,
Those shambling legs, and gouty toes ;
Thus form'd to snore throughout the day,—
And eat and drink the night away ;

I ne'er had felt the fev'rish flame
That caus'd my bloody thirst for fame;
Nor madly claim'd immortal birth,
Because the vilest brute on Earth:
And, oh! I'd not been doom'd to hear,
Still whizzing in my blister'd ear,
The curses deep, in damning peals,
That rose from 'neath my chariot wheels,
When I along the embattled plain
With furious triumph crush'd the slain:
I should not thus be doom'd to see,
In every shape of agony,
The victims of my cruel wrath,
For ever dying, strew my path;
The grinding teeth, the lips awry,
The inflated nose, the starting eye,
The mangled bodies writhing round,
Like serpents, on the bloody ground;

Is hould not thus for ever seem
A charnel house, and scent the steam
Of black, fermenting, putrid gore,
Rank oozing through each burning pore;
Behold, as on a dungeon wall,
The worms upon my body crawl,
The which, if I would brush away,
Around my clammy fingers play,
And, twining fast with many a coil,
In loathsome sport my labor foil.

Enough! the frighted Painter cried,
And hung his head in fallen pride.

Not so the other. He, of stuff
More stubborn, ne'er would cry enough;
But like a soundly cudgell'd oak,
More sturdy grew at every stroke,

And thus again his ready tongue
With fluent logick would have rung:
My Lord, I'll prove, or I'm a liar—
Whom interrupting then with ire,
Thus check'd the Judge: Oh, proud yet mean!
And canst thou hope from me to screen
Thy foolish heart, and o'er it spread
A veil to cheat th' omniscient dead?
And canst thou hope, as once on Earth,
Applause to gain by specious worth;
Like those that still by sneer and taunt
Would prove pernicious what they want;
And claim the mastership of Art,
Because thou only know'st a *part*?

Had'st thou from Nature, not the Schools
Distorted by pedantic rules,
With patience wrought, such logic vain
Had ne'er perverted thus thy brain:

For Genius never gave delight
By means of what offends the sight:
Nor hadst thou deem'd, with folly mad,
Thou could'st to Nature's beauties *add*,
By *taking from her that which gives*
The best assurance that she lives;
By imperfection give attraction,
And multiply them by subtraction.

Did Raffaelle thus, whose honour'd ghost
Is now Elysium's fairest boast?
Far diff'rent He. Though weak and lame
In parts that gave to others fame,
Yet sought not *he* by such defect
To swindle praise for *wise neglect*
Of *vulgar* charms, that only *blind*
The dazzled eye to those of Mind.
By Heaven impress'd with Genius' seal,
An eye to see, and heart to feel,

His soul through boundless Nature rov'd,
And seeing felt, and feeling lov'd.
But weak the power of mind at will
To give the hand the painter's skill;
For mortal works, maturing slow,
From patient care and labour flow:
And hence restrain'd, his youthful hand
Obey'd a master's dull command;
But soon with health his sickly style
From Leonardo learn'd to smile;
And now from Bonaroti caught
A nobler Form; and now it sought
Of colour fair the magic spell,
And trac'd her to the Friar's* cell.
No foolish pride, no narrow rule
Enslav'd his soul; from every School,

* Fra. Bartolomeo.

Whatever fair, whatever grand,
His pencil, like a potent wand,
Transfusing, bade his canvass grace.
Progressive thus, with giant pace,
And energy no toil could tame,
He climb'd the rugged mount of Fame:
And soon had reach'd the summit bold,
When Death, who there delights to hold
His fatal watch, with envious blow
Quick hurl'd him to the shades below.

Thus check'd the Judge the champion vain
Of *Classic Form;* and thus in strain,
By anger half and pity mov'd,
The ghostly Colourist reprov'd.
And what didst *Thou* aspire to gain,
Who dar'd'st the will of Jove arraign,
That bounded thus within a span
The little life of little man;

With shallow art deriving thence
Excuses for thy indolence ?
'Tis cant and hypocritic stuff!
The life of man is long enough :
For did he but the half improve
He would not quarrel thus with Jove.

But most I marvel (if it be
That aught may wond'rous seem to me)
That Jove's high Gift, your noble Art,
Bestow'd to raise Man's grov'ling heart,
Refining with ethereal ray
Each gross and selfish thought away,
Should pander turn of paltry pelf,
Imprisoning each within himself;
Or like a gorgeous serpent, be
Your splendid source of misery,
And, crushing with his burnish'd folds,
Still narrower make your narrow souls.

But words can ne'er reform produce,
In Ignorance and Pride obtuse.
Then know, ye vain and foolish Pair!
Your doom is fix'd a yoke to bear
Like beasts on Earth; and, thus in tether,
Five Centuries to paint together.
If, thus by mutual labours join'd,
Your jarring souls should be combin'd,
The faults of each the other mending,
The powers of both harmonious blending;
Great Jove, perhaps, in gracious vein,
May send your souls on Earth again;
Yet there One only Painter be;
For thus the eternal Fates decree:
One Leg alone shall never run,
Nor two Half-Painters make but One.

ECCENTRICITY.

ECCENTRICITY.

Projecere animas. VIRG.

ALAS, my friend! what hope have I of fame,
Who am, as Nature made me, still the same?
And thou, poor suitor to a bankrupt muse,
How mad thy toil, how arrogant thy views!
What though endued with Genius' power to move
The magick chords of sympathy and love,
The painter's eye, the poet's fervid heart,
The tongue of eloquence, the vital art
Of bold Prometheus, kindling at command
With breathing life the labours of his hand;
Yet shall the World thy daring high pretence
With scorn deride, for thou—hast common sense.

But dost thou, reckless of stern honour's laws,
Intemperate hunger for the World's applause?
Bid Nature hence; her fresh embow'ring woods,
Her lawns and fields, and rocks, and rushing floods,
And limpid lakes, and health-exhaling soil,
Elastick gales, and all the glorious toil
Of Heaven's own hand, with courtly shame discard,
And Fame shall triumph in her city bard.
Then, pent secure in some commodious lane,
Where stagnant Darkness holds her morbid reign,
Perchance snug-roosted o'er some brazier's den,
Or stall of nymphs, by courtesy *not* men,
Whose gentle trade to skin the living eel,
The while they curse it that it dares to feel*;
Whilst ribbald jokes and repartees proclaim
Their happy triumph o'er the sense of shame;

* See Boswell's Life of Johnson.

Thy city Muse invoke, that imp of mind
By smoke engender'd on an eastern wind;
Then, half-awake, thy patent-thinking pen
The paper give, and blot the souls of men.

The time has been when Nature's simple face
Perennial youth possess'd and winning grace;
But who shall dare, in this refining age,
With Nature's praise to soil his snowy page?
What polish'd lover, unappall'd by sneers,
Dare court a beldame of six thousand years,
When every clown with microscopick eyes
The gaping furrows on her forehead spies?—
'Good sir, your pardon: In her naked state,
Her wither'd form we cannot chuse but hate;
But fashion's art the waste of time repairs,
Each wrinkle fills, and dies her silver hairs;
Thus wrought anew, our gentle bosoms low;
We cannot chuse but love what's *comme il faut.*'

Alas, poor Cowper! could thy chasten'd eye,
(Awhile forgetful of thy joys on high)
Revisit earth, what indignation strange
Would sting thee to behold the courtly change!
Here "velvet" lawns, there "plushy" woods that lave
Their "silken" tresses in the "glassy" wave;
Here "'broider'd" meads, there flow'ry "carpets" spread,
And "downy" banks to "pillow" Nature's head;
How wouldst thou start to find thy native soil,
Like birth-day belle, by gross mechanick toil
Trick'd out to charm with meretricious air,
As though all France and Manchester were there!
But this were luxury, were bliss refin'd,
To view the alter'd region of the mind;
Where whim and mystery, like wizards, rule,
And conjure wisdom from the seeming fool;
Where learned heads, like old cremonas, boast
Their merit soundest that are cracked the most;

While Genius' self, infected with the joke,
His person decks with Folly's motley cloak.

Behold, loud-rattling like a thousand drums,
Eccentrick Hal, the child of Nature, comes!
Of Nature once—but *now* he acts a part,
And Hal is now the full grown boy of art.
In youth's pure spring his high impetuous soul
Nor custom own'd nor fashion's vile control.
By Truth impell'd where beck'ning Nature led,
Through life he mov'd with firm elastic tread;
But soon the world, with wonder-teeming eyes,
His manners mark, and goggle with surprise.
"He's wond'rous strange!" exclaims each gaping clod,
"A wond'rous genius, for he's wond'rous odd!"
Where'er he goes, there goes before his fame,
And courts and taverns echo round his name;

'Till, fairly knock'd by admiration down,
The petted monster cracks his wond'rous crown.
No longer now to simple Nature true,
He studies only to be oddly new;
Whate'er he does, whate'er he deigns to say,
Must all be said and done the oddest way;
Nay, e'en in dress eccentrick as in thought,
His wardrobe seems by Lapland witches wrought,
Himself by goblins in a whirlwind drest
With rags of clouds from Hecla's stormy crest.

'Has Truth no charms?' When first beheld, I grant,
But, wanting novelty, has every want:
For pleasure's thrill the sickly palate flies,
Save haply pungent with a rare surprise.
The humble toad that leaps her nightly round,
The harmless tenant of the garden ground,

Is loath'd, abhor'd, nay, all the reptile race
Together join'd were never half so base ;
Yet snugly find her in some quarry pent,
Through ages doom'd to one tremendous lent,
Surviving still, as if "in Nature's spite,"
Without or nourishment, or air, or light,
What raptures then th' astonish'd gazer seize !
What lovely creature like a toad can please !

Hence many an oaf, by Nature doom'd to shine
The unknown father of an unknown line,
If haply shipwreck'd on some desert shore
Of Folly's seas, by man untrod before,
Which, bleak and barren, to the starving mind
Yields nought but fog, or damp, unwholesome wind,
With loud applause the wond'ring world shall hail,
And Fame embalm him in the marv'lous tale.

With chest erect, and bright uplifted eye,
On tiptoe rais'd, like one prepar'd to fly,
Yon wight behold, whose sole aspiring hope
Eccentrick soars to catch the hangman's rope.
In order rang'd, with date of place and time,
Each owner's name, his parentage and crime,
High on his walls, inscribed to glorious shame,
Unnumber'd halters gibbet him to Fame.

Who next appears thus stalking by his side?
Why that is one who'd sooner die than—ride!
No inch of ground can maps unheard of show
Untrac'd by him, unknown to every toe:
As if intent this punning age to suit,
The globe's circumf'rence meas'ring by the foot.

Nor less renown'd whom stars invet'rate doom
To smiles eternal, or eternal gloom;

For what's a *character* save one confin'd
To some unchanging sameness of the mind;
To some strange, fix'd monotony of mien,
Or dress forever brown, forever green?

A sample comes. Observe his sombre face,
Twin-born with Death, without his brother's grace!
No joy in mirth his soul perverted knows,
Whose only joy to tell of others' woes.
A fractur'd limb, a conflagrating fire,
A name or fortune lost his tongue inspire:
From house to house where'er misfortunes press,
Like Fate, he roams, and revels in distress;
In every ear with dismal boding moans—
A walking register of sighs and groans!

High tow'ring next, as he'd eclipse the moon,
With pride upblown, behold yon live balloon.

All trades above, all sciences and arts,
To fame he climbs through very scorn of parts;
With solemn emptiness distends his state,
And, great in nothing, soars above the great;
Nay stranger still, through apathy of blood,
By candour number'd with the chaste and good:
With wife, and child, domestic, stranger, friend,
Alike he lives, as though his being's end
Were o'er his house like formal guest to roam,
And walk abroad to leave himself at home.

But who is he, that sweet obliging youth?
He looks the picture of ingenuous truth.
Oh, that's his antipode, of courteous race,
The man of bows and ever-smiling face.
Why Nature made him, or for what design'd,
Never he knew, nor ever sought to find,
'Till cunning came, blest harbinger of ease!
And kindly whisper'd, 'thou wert born to please.'

Rous'd by the news, behold him now expand,
Like beaten gold, and glitter o'er the land.
Well stored with nods and sly approving winks,
Now first with this and now with that he thinks;
Howe'er opposing, still assents to each,
And claps a dovetail to each booby's speech.
At random thus for all, for none, he lives,
Profusely lavish though he nothing gives;
The world he roves as living but to show
A friendless man without a single foe;
From bad to good, to bad from good to run,
And find a character by seeking none.

Who covets fame should ne'er be over nice,
Some slight distortion pays the market price.
If haply lam'd by some propitious chance,
Instruct in attitude, or teach to dance;
Be still extravagant in deed, or word;
If new, enough, no matter how absurd.

Then what is Genius? Nay, if rightly us'd,
Some gift of Nature happily abus'd.
Nor wrongly deem by this eccentrick rule
That Nature favours whom she makes a fool;
Her scorn and favour we alike despise;
Not Nature's follies but our own we prize.

"Or what is wit?" a meteor bright and rare,
What comes and goes we know not whence, or where;
A brilliant nothing out of something wrought,
A mental vacuum by condensing thought.

Behold Tortoso. There's a man of wit;
To all things fitted, though for nothing fit;
Scourge of the world, yet crouching for a name,
And honour bartering for the breath of fame:
Born to command, and yet an arrant slave;
Through too much honesty a seeming knave;

At all things grasping, though on nothing bent,
And ease pursuing e'en with discontent;
Through Nature, Arts, and Sciences he flies,
And gathers truth to manufacture lies.

Nor only Wits, for tortur'd talents claim
Of sov'reign mobs the glorious meed of fame;
E'en Sages too, of grave and rev'rend air,
Yclepp'd *Philosophers*, must have their share;
Who deeper still in conjuration skill'd,
A mighty something out of nothing build.

'Then wherefore read? why cram the youthful head
With all the learned lumber of the dead;
Who seeking wisdom follow'd Nature's laws,
Nor dar'd effects admit without a cause?'
Why?—Ask the sophist of our modern school;
To foil the workman we must know the tool;

And, that possess'd, how swiftly is defac'd
The noblest, rarest monument of taste !
So neatly too, the mutilations stand
Like native errors of the artist's hand;
Nay, what is more, the very tool betray'd
To seem the product of the work it made.

'Oh, monstrous slander on the human race !'
Then read conviction in Ortuno's case.
By Nature fashion'd in her happiest mood,
With learning, fancy, keenest wit endued ;
To what high purpose, what exalted end
These lofty gifts did great Ortuno bend?
With grateful triumph did Ortuno raise
The mighty trophies to their Author's praise ;
With skill deducing from th' harmonious whole
Immortal proofs of One Creative soul ?
Ah, no ! infatuate with the dazzling light,
In them he saw their own creative might ;

Nay, madly deem'd, if *such* their wond'rous *skill*,
The phantom of a God 'twas theirs to *will.*

But granting that he *is*, he bids you show
By what you prove it, or by what you know.
Oh, reas'ning worm! who questions thus of Him
That lives in all, and moves in every limb,
Must with himself in very strangeness dwell,
Has never heard the voice of Conscience tell
Of right and wrong, and speak in louder tone
Than tropick thunder of that Holy One,
Whose pure, eternal, justice shall require
The deed of wrong, and justify the right.

Can such blaspheme and breathe the vital air?
Let mad philosophy their names declare.
Yet some there are, less daring in their aim,
With humbler cunning butcher sense for fame;

Who doubting still, with many a fearful pause,
Th' existence grant of one almighty cause;
But halting there, in bolder tone deny
The life hereafter, when the man shall die,
Nor mark the monstrous folly of their gain—
That God all-wise should fashion *them* in vain.

'Twere labour lost in this material age,
When school boys trample on the Inspir'd Page,
When coblers prove by syllogistick pun
The soal they mend, and that of man are one;
'Twere waste of time to check the Muses' speed,
For all the *whys* and *wherefores* of their creed;
To show how prov'd the juices are the same
That feed the body, and the mental frame.

But who, half sceptic, half afraid of wrong,
Shall walk our streets, and mark the passing
throng;

The brawny oaf in mould herculean cast,
The pigmy statesman trembling in his blast,
The cumb'rous citizen of portly paunch,
Unwont to soar beyond the smoaking haunch;
The meagre bard behind the moving tun,
His shadow seeming lengthen'd by the sun;
Who forms scarce visible shall thus descry,
Like flitting clouds athwart the mental sky;
From giant bodies then bare gleams of mind,
Like mountain watch-lights blinking to the wind;
Nor blush to find his unperverted eye
Flash on his heart, and give his tongue the lie.

'Tis passing strange! yet, born as if to show
Man to himself his most malignant foe,
There are (so desperate is the madness grown)
Who'd rather live a *lie* than live unknown;
Whose very tongues, with force of holy writ,
Their doctrines damn with self-recoiling wit.

Behold yon dwarf, of visage pale and wan ;
A sketch of life, a remnant of a man !
Whose livid lips, as now he moulds a grin,
Like charnel doors disclose the waste within ;
Whose stiffen'd joints within their sockets grind,
Like gibbets creaking to the passing wind ;
Whose shrivell'd skin with much adhesion clings
His bones around in hard compacted rings,
If veins there were, no blood beneath could force,
Unless by miracle, its trickling course ;—
Yet even *he* within that sapless frame,
A mind sustain'd that climb'd the steeps of fame.
Such is the form by mystic Heaven design'd,
The earthly mansion of the rarest mind.
But, mark his gratitude. This soul sublime,
This soul lord paramount o'er space and time,
This soul of fire, with impious madness sought,
Itself to prove of mortal matter wrought ;

Nay, bred, engender'd, on the grub-worm plan,
From that vile clay which made his outward man,
That shadowy form which dark'ning into birth,
But seem'd a sign to mark a soul on earth.

But who shall cast an introverted eye
Upon himself, that will not there descry
A conscious life that shall, nor cannot die?
E'en at our birth, when first the infant mould
Gives it a mansion and an earthly hold,
Th' exulting Spirit feels the heavenly fire
That lights her tenement will ne'er expire;
And when, in after years, disease and age,
Our fellow-bodies sweeping from life's stage,
Obtrude the thought of death, e'en then we seem,
As in the revelation of a dream,
To hear a voice, more audible than speech,
Warn of a part which death can never reach.

Survey the tribes of savage men that roam
Like wand'ring herds, each wilderness their home ;—
Nay, even there th' immortal spirit stands
Firm on the verge of death, and looks to brighter
lands.

Shall human wisdom then, with beetle sight,
Because obstructed in its blund'ring flight,
Despise the deep conviction of our birth,
And limit life to this degraded earth ?

Oh, far from me be that insatiate pride,
Which, turning on itself, drinks up the tide
Of natural light; 'till one eternal gloom,
Like walls of adamant enclose the tomb.
Tremendous thought! that this transcendant
Power,
Fell'd with the body in one fatal hour,
With all its faculties, should pass like air
For ages without end as though it never were !

Say, whence, obedient, to their destin'd end
The various tribes of living nature tend?
Why beast, and bird, and all the countless race
Of earth and waters, each his proper place
Instinctive knows, and through the endless chain
Of being moves in one harmonious strain;
While man alone, with strange perversion, draws
Rebellious fame from Nature's broken laws?
Methinks I hear, in that still voice which stole
On Horeb's mount o'er rapt Elijah's soul,
With stern reproof indignant Heaven reply:
'Tis o'erweening Pride, that blinds the eye
Of reasoning man, and o'er his darken'd life
Confusion spreads and misery and strife.

With wonder fill'd and self-reflecting praise,
The slave of pride his mighty powers surveys;
On Reason's sun (by bounteous Nature given,
To guide the soul upon her way to heaven)

Adoring gazes, 'till the dazzling light,
To darkness sears his vain presumptuous sight;
Then bold, though blind, through error's night
he runs,
In fancy lighted by a thousand suns;
For bloody laurels now the warrior plays,
Now libels nature for the poet's bays;
Now darkness drinks from metaphysic springs,
Or follows fate on astrologick wings:
'Mid toils at length the world's loud wonder won,
With Persian piety, to Reason's sun
Profound he bows, and, idolist of fame,
Forgets the God who lighted first the flame.

All potent Reason! what thy wond'rous light?
A shooting star athwart a polar night;
A bubble's gleam amid the boundless main;
A sparkling sand on waste Arabia's plain:

E'en such, vain Power, thy limited control,
E'en such thou art, to mans mysterious soul!

Presumptuous man! would'st thou aspiring reach
True wisdom's height, let conscious weakness
teach
Thy feeble soul her poor dependant state,
Nor madly war with Nature to be great.

Come then, Humility, thou surest guide!
On earth again with frenzied men reside;
Tear the dark film of vanity and lies,
And inward turn their renovated eyes;
In aspect true let each himself behold,
By self deform'd in pride's portentous mould.
And if thy voice, on Bethl'em's holy plain
Once heard, can reach their flinty hearts again,
Teach them, as fearful of a serpent's gaze,
Teach them to shun the gloating eye of praise;

That slightest swervings from their nature's plan
Make them a lie, and poison all the man,
'Till black corruption spread the soul throughout,
Whence thick and fierce, like fabled mandrakes, sprout
The seeds of vice with more than tropick force,
Exhausting in the growth their very vital source.

Nor wrongly deem the cynick muse aspires,
With monkish tears to quench our nobler fires.
Let honest pride our humble hearts inflame,
First to deserve, ere yet we look to, fame;
Not fame miscall'd, the mob's applauding stare;
This monsters have, proportion'd as they're rare;
But that sweet praise, the tribute of the good,
For wisdom gain'd, through love of truth pursued.
Coeval with our birth, this pure desire
Was given to lift our grov'ling natures higher,

Till that high praise, by genuine merit wrung
From men's slow justice, shall employ the tongue
Of yon Supernal Court, from whom may flow
Or bliss eternal or eternal wo.
And since in all this hope exalting lives,
Let virtuous toil improve what Nature gives:
Each in his sphere some glorious palm may gain,
For Heaven all-wise created nought in vain.

Oh, task sublime, to till the human soil
Where fruits immortal crown the lab'ror's toil!
Where deathless flowers, in everlasting bloom,
May gales from Heaven with odorous sweets perfume;
Whose fragrance still when man's last work is done,
And hoary Time his final course has run,
Thro' ages back, with fresh'ning power shall last,
Mark his long track, and linger where he past!

THE

PAINT-KING.

THE
PAINT-KING.

FAIR Ellen was long the delight of the young,
No damsel could with her compare ;
Her charms were the theme of the heart and the tongue,
And bards without number in extacies sung,
The beauties of Ellen the fair.

Yet cold was the maid; and tho' legions advanc'd,
All drill'd by Ovidean art,
And languish'd, and ogled, protested and danced,
Like shadows they came, and like shadows they glanced
From the hard polish'd ice of her heart.

Yet still did the heart of fair Ellen implore
A something that could not be found;
Like a sailor she seem'd on a desolate shore,
With nor house, nor a tree, nor a sound but the roar
Of breakers high dashing around.

From object to object still, still would she veer,
Though nothing, alas, could she find;
Like the moon, without atmosphere, brilliant and clear,
Yet doom'd, like the moon, with no being to cheer
The bright barren waste of her mind.

But rather than sit like a statue so still
When the rain made her mansion a *pound*,
Up and down would she go, like the sails of a mill,
And pat every stair, like a woodpecker's bill,
From the tiles of the roof to the ground.

One morn, as the maid from her casement inclin'd,
Pass'd a youth, with a frame in his hand.
The casement she clos'd—not the eye of her mind;
For, do all she could, no, she could not be blind;
Still before her she saw the youth stand.

"Ah, what can he do," said the languishing maid,
"Ah, what with that frame can he do?"
And she knelt to the Goddess of Secrets and pray'd,
When the youth pass'd again, and again he display'd
The frame and a picture to view.

"Oh, beautiful picture!" the fair Ellen cried,
"I must see thee again or I die."
Then under her white chin her bonnet she tied,
And after the youth and the picture she hied,
When the youth, looking back, met her eye.

" Fair damsel," said he (and he chuckled the
while)
" This picture I see you admire :
Then take it, I pray you, perhaps 'twill beguile
Some moments of sorrow; (nay, pardon my
smile)
Or, at least, keep you home by the fire."

Then Ellen the gift with delight and surprise
From the cunning young stripling receiv'd.
But she knew not the poison that enter'd her eyes,
When sparkling with rapture they gaz'd on her
prize—
Thus, alas, are fair maidens deceiv'd!

'Twas a youth o'er the form of a statue inclin'd,
And the sculptor he seem'd of the stone;
Yet he languish'd as tho' for its beauty he pin'd
And gaz'd as the eyes of the statue so blind
Reflected the beams of his own.

'Twas the tale of the sculptor Pygmalion of old;
Fair Ellen remember'd, and sigh'd;
" Ah, could'st thou but lift from that marble so
cold,
Thine eyes too imploring, thy arms should enfold,
And press me this day as thy bride."

She said: when, behold, from the canvass arose
The youth, and he stepp'd from the frame:
With a furious transport his arms did enclose
The love-plighted Ellen: and, clasping, he froze
The blood of the maid with his flame!

She turn'd and beheld on each shoulder a wing.
" Oh, heaven! cried she, who art thou?"
From the roof to the ground did his fierce an-
swer ring,
As frowning, he thunder'd " I am the PAINT-
KING!
And mine, lovely maid, thou art now!"

Then high from the ground did the grim monster lift
The loud-screaming maid like a blast;
And he sped through the air like a meteor swift,
While the clouds, wand'ring by him, did fearfully drift
To the right and the left as he pass'd.

Now suddenly sloping his hurricane flight,
With an eddying whirl he descends;
The air all below him becomes black as night,
And the ground where he treads, as if mov'd with affright,
Like the surge of the Caspian bends.

"I am here!" said the Fiend, and he thundering knock'd
At the gates of a mountainous cave;
The gates open flew, as by magick unlock'd,
While the peaks of the mount, reeling to and fro, rock'd
Like an island of ice on the wave.

"Oh, mercy!" cried Ellen, and swoon'd in his arms,
But the PAINT-KING, he scoff'd at her pain.
"Prithee, love," said the monster, "what mean these alarms?"
She hears not, she sees not the terrible charms,
That work her to horrour again.

She opens her lids, but no longer her eyes
Behold the fair youth she would woo;
Now appears the PAINT-KING in his natural guise;
His face, like a palette of villainous dies,
Black and white, red, and yellow, and blue.

On the skull of a Titan, that Heaven defied,
Sat the fiend, like the grim Giant Gog,
While aloft to his mouth a huge pipe he applied,
Twice as big as the Eddystone Lighthouse, descried
As it looms through an easterly fog.

And anon, as he puff'd the vast volumes, were seen,
In horrid festoons on the wall,
Legs and arms, heads and bodies emerging be-
tween,
Like the drawing-room grim of the Scotch Saw-
ney Beane,
By the Devil dress'd out for a ball.

" Ah me !" cried the Damsel, and fell at his feet.
" Must I hang on these walls to be dried?"
" Oh, no !" said the fiend, while he sprung from
his seat,
" A far nobler fortune thy person shall meet;
Into paint will I grind thee, my bride !"

Then, seizing the maid by her dark auburn hair,
An oil jug he plung'd her within.
Seven days seven nights, with the shrieks of des-
pair,
Did Ellen in torment convulse the dun air,
All covered with oil to the chin.

On the morn of the eighth on a huge sable stone
Then Ellen, all reeking, he laid;
With a rock for his muller he crush'd every bone,
But, though ground to jelly, still, still did she
groan;
For life had forsook not the maid.

Now reaching his palette, with masterly care
Each tint on its surface he spread;
The blue of her eyes, and the brown of her hair,
And the pearl and the white of her forehead so
fair,
And her lips' and her cheeks' rosy red.

Then, stamping his foot, did the monster exclaim,
"Now I brave, cruel Fairy, thy scorn!"
When lo! from a chasm wide-yawning there came
A light tiny chariot of rose-colour'd flame,
By a team of ten glow-worms upborne.

Enthron'd in the midst on an emerald bright,
Fair Geraldine sat without peer;
Her robe was a gleam of the first blush of light,
And her mantle the fleece of a noon-cloud white,
And a beam of the moon was her spear.

In an accent that stole on the still charmed air
Like the first gentle language of Eve,
Thus spake from her chariot the Fairy so fair:
" I come at thy call, but, oh Paint-King, beware,
Beware if again you deceive."

" 'Tis true," said the monster, " thou queen of
my heart,
Thy portrait I oft have essay'd;
Yet ne'er to the canvass could I with my art
The least of thy wonderful beauties impart;
And my failure with scorn you repaid.

" Now I swear by the light of the Comet-King's
tail!"
And he tower'd with pride as he spoke,
" If again with these magical colours I fail,
The crater of Etna shall hence be my jail,
And my food shall be sulphur and smoke.

" But if I succeed, then, oh, fair Geraldine!
Thy promise with justice I claim,
And thou, queen of Fairies, shalt ever be mine,
The bride of my bed; and thy portrait divine
Shall fill all the earth with my fame."

He spake; when, behold, the fair Geraldine's
form
On the canvass enchantingly glow'd;
His touches—they flew like the leaves in a storm;
And the pure pearly white and the carnation
warm
Contending in harmony flow'd.

And now did the portrait a twin-sister seem
To the figure of Geraldine fair :
With the same sweet expression did faithfully teem
Each muscle; each feature; in short not a gleam
Was lost of her beautiful hair.

Twas the Fairy herself! but, alas, her blue eyes
Still a pupil did ruefully lack ;
And who shall describe the terrifick surprise
That seiz'd the PAINT-KING when, behold, he descries
Not a speck on his palette of black !

" I am lost!" said the Fiend, and he shook like a leaf ;
When, casting his eyes to the ground,
He saw the lost pupils of Ellen with grief
In the jaws of a mouse, and the sly little thief
Whisk away from his sight with a bound.

" I am lost!" said the Fiend, and he fell like a stone;
Then rising the Fairy in ire
With a touch of her finger she loosen'd her zone,
(While the limbs on the wall gave a terrible
groan,)
And she swelled to a column of fire.

Her spear now a thunder-bolt flash'd in the air,
And sulphur the vault fill'd around :
She smote the grim monster ; and now by the hair
High-lifting, she hurl'd him in speechless despair
Down the depths of the chasm profound.

Then over the picture thrice waving her spear,
" Come forth !" said the good Geraldine ;
When, behold, from the canvass descending, ap-
pear
Fair Ellen, in person more lovely than e'er,
With grace more than ever divine !

MYRTILLA.

MYRTILLA.

Addressed to a LADY, who lamented that she had never been in love.

" Al nuovo giorno,
Pietosa man' mi sollevo.

METASTASIO.

" Ah me! how sad," Myrtilla cried,
" To waste alone my years!"
While o'er a streamlet's flow'ry side
She pensive hung, and watch'd the tide
That dimpled with her tears.

" The world, though oft to merit blind,
Alas, I cannot blame ;
For they have oft the knee inclined,
And pour'd the sigh—but, like the wind
Of winter, cold it came.

" Ah no ! neglect I cannot rue."
Then o'er the limpid stream
She cast her eyes of ether blue ;
Her wat'ry eyes look'd up to view
Their lovelier parent's beam.

And ever as the sad lament
Would thus her lips divide,
Her lips, like sister roses bent
By passing gales, elastick sent
Their blushes from the tide.

While mournful o'er her pictur'd face
Did then her glances steal,
She seem'd she thought a marble Grace,
T' enslave with love the human race,
But ne'er that love to feel.

" Ah, what avail those eyes replete
With charms without a name !
Alas, no kindred rays they meet,
To kindle by collision sweet
Of mutual love the flame !

" Oh, 'tis the worst of cruel things,
This solitary state !
Yon bird that trims his purple wings,
As on the bending bow he swings,
Prepares to join his mate.

" The little glow-worm sheds her light,
 Nor sheds her light in vain—
That still her tiny lover's sight
Amid the darkness of the night
 May trace her o'er the plain.

" All living nature seems to move
 By sympathy divine—
The sea, the earth, the air above ;
As if one universal love
 Did all their hearts entwine !

" My heart alone of all my kind
 No love can ever warm :
That only can resemblance find
With waste Arabia, where the wind
 Ne'er breathes on human form ;

" A blank, embodied space, that knows
No changes in its reign,
Save when the fierce tornado throws
Its barren sands, like drifted snows,
In ridges o'er the plain."

Thus plain'd the maid; and now her eyes
Slow-lifting from the tide,
Their liquid orbs with sweet surprise
A youth beheld in extacies,
Mute standing by her side.

" Forbear, oh, lovely maid, forbear,"
The youth enamour'd cried,
" Nor with Arabia's waste compare
The heart of one so young and fair,
To every charm allied.

"Or, if Arabia—rather say,
    Where some delicious spring
Remurmurs to the leaves that play
Mid palm and date and flow'ret gay,
    On zephyr's frolick wing.

"And now, methinks, I cannot deem
    The picture else but true;
For I a wand'ring trav'ller seem
O'er life's drear waste, without a gleam
    Of hope—if not in *you*."

Thus spake the youth; and then his tongue
    Such converse sweet distill'd,
It seem'd, as on his words she hung,
As though a heavenly spirit sung,
    And all her soul he fill'd.

He told her of his cruel fate,
Condemn'd alone to rove,
From infancy to man's estate,
Though courted by the fair and great,
Yet never once to love.

And then from many a poet's page
The blest reverse he proved :
How sweet to pass life's pilgrimage,
From purple youth to sere old age,
Aye loving and beloved !

Here ceased the youth ; but still his words
Did o'er her fancy play ;
They seem'd the matin song of birds,
Or like the distant low of herds
That welcomes in the day.

The sympathetick chord she feels
Soft thrilling in her soul;
And, as the sweet vibration steals
Through every vein, in tender peals
She seems to hear it roll.

Her alter'd heart, of late so drear,
Then seem'd a faery land,
Where nymphs and rosy loves appear
On margin green of fountain clear,
And frolick hand in hand.

But who shall paint her crimson blush,
Nor think his hand of stone,
As now the secret with a flush
Did o'er her aching senses rush—
Her heart was not her own!

The happy Lindor, with a look
    That every hope confess'd,
Her glowing hand exulting took,
And press'd it, as she fearful shook,
    In silence to his breast.

Myrtilla felt the spreading flame,
    Yet knew not how to chide;
So sweet it mantled o'er her frame,
That, with a smile of pride and shame,
    She own'd herself his bride.

No longer then, ye fair, complain,
    And call the fates unkind;
The high, the low, the meek, the vain,
Shall each a sympathetick swain,
    Another *self* shall find.

TO A LADY

Who spoke slightingly of Poets.

Oh, censure not the Poet's art,
Nor think it chills the feeling heart
    To love the gentle Muses.
Can that which in a stone or flower,
As if by transmigrating power,
    His gen'rous soul infuses;

Can that for social joys impair
The heart that like the lib'ral air
    All Nature's self embraces;
That in the cold Norwegian main,
Or mid the tropic hurricane
    Her varied beauty traces;

That in her meanest work can find
A fitness and a grace combin'd
In blest harmonious union,
That even with the cricket holds,
As if by sympathy of souls,
Mysterious communion;

Can that with sordid selfishness
His wide-expanded heart impress,
Whose consciousness is loving;
Who, giving life to all he spies,
His joyous being multiplies,
In youthfulness improving?

Oh, Lady, then, fair queen of Earth,
Thou loveliest of mortal birth,
Spurn not thy truest lover;
Nor censure *him* whose keener sense
Can feel thy magic influence
Where nought the world discover;

Whose eye on that bewitching face
Can every source unnumber'd trace
Of germinating blisses;
See Sylphids o'er thy forehead weave
The lily-fibred film, and leave
It fix'd with honied kisses;

While some within thy liquid eyes,
Like minnows of a thousand dies
Through lucid waters glancing,
In busy motion to and fro,
The gems of diamond-beetles sow,
Their lustre thus enhancing;

Here some, their little vases fill'd
With blushes for thy cheek distill'd
From roses newly blowing,
Each tiny thirsting pore supply;
And some in quick succession by
The down of peaches strewing:

There others who from hanging bell
Of cowslip caught the dew that fell
While yet the day was breaking,
And o'er thy pouting lips diffuse
The tincture—still its glowing hues
Of purple morn partaking :

Here some, that in the petals prest
Of humid honeysuckles, rest
From nightly fog defended,
Flutter their fragrant wings between,
Like humming-birds that scarce are seen,
They seem with air so blended !

While some, in equal clusters knit,
On either side in circles flit,
Like bees in April swarming,
Their tiny weight each other lend,
And force the yielding cheek to bend,
Thy laughing dimples forming.

Nor, Lady, think the Poet's eye
Can only outward charms espy,
  Thy form alone adoring—
Ah, Lady, no: though fair they be,
Yet he a fairer sight may see,
  Thy lovely *soul* exploring:

And while from part to part it flies
The gentle Spirit he descries,
  Through every line pursuing;
And feels upon his nature shower
That pure, that humanizing power,
  Which raises by subduing.

SONNET

On a Falling Group in the Last Judgement of MICHAEL ANGELO, *in the Cappella Sistina.*

How vast, how dread, o'erwhelming is the thought
Of Space interminable! to the soul
A circling weight that crushes into nought
Her mighty faculties! a wond'rous whole,
Without or parts, beginning, or an end!
How fearful then on desp'rate wings to send
The fancy e'en amid the waste profound!
Yet, born as if all daring to astound,
Thy giant hand, oh Angelo, hath hurl'd
E'en human forms, with all their mortal weight,
Down the dread void—fall endless as their fate!
Already now they seem from world to world
For ages thrown; yet doom'd, another past,
Another still to reach, nor e'er to reach the last!

SONNET

On the Group of the Three Angels before the Tent of Abraham, by RAFFAELLE, *in the Vatican.*

OH, now I feel as though another sense
From Heaven descending had inform'd my soul;
I feel the pleasurable, full control
Of Grace, harmonious, boundless, and intense.
In thee, celestial Group, embodied lives
The subtle mystery; that speaking gives
Itself resolv'd: the essences combin'd
Of Motion ceaseless, Unity complete.
Borne like a leaf by some soft eddying wind,
Mine eyes, impell'd as by enchantment sweet,
From part to part with circling motion rove,
Yet seem unconscious of the power to move;
From line to line through endless changes run,
O'er countless shapes, yet seem to gaze on One.

SONNET

On seeing the Picture of Æolus by PELIGRI-NO TIBALDI, *in the Institute at Bologna.*

FULL well, Tibaldi, did thy kindred mind
The mighty spell of Bonarroti own.
Like one who, reading magick words, receives
The gift of intercourse with worlds uknnown,
'Twas thine, decyph'ring Nature's mystick leaves,
To hold strange converse with the viewless wind;
To see the Spirits, in embodied forms,
Of gales and whirlwinds, hurricanes and storms.
For, lo! obedient to thy bidding, teems
Fierce into shape their stern relentless Lord:
His form of motion ever-restless seems;
Or, if to rest inclin'd his turbid soul,
On Hecla's top to stretch, and give the word
To subject Winds that sweep the desert pole.

SONNET

On Rembrant; occasioned by his Picture of Jacob's Dream.

As in that twilight, superstitious age
When all beyond the narrow grasp of mind
Seem'd fraught with meanings of supernal kind,
When e'en the learned philosophic sage,
Wont with the stars thro' boundless space to range,
Listen'd with rev'rence to the changeling's tale;
E'en so, thou strangest of all beings strange!
E'en so thy visionary scenes I hail;
That like the ramblings of an idiot's speech,
No image giving of a thing on earth,
Nor thought significant in Reason's reach,
Yet in their random shadowings give birth
To thoughts and things from other worlds that come,
And fill the soul, and strike the reason dumb.

SONNET

On the Luxembourg Gallery.

THERE is a Charm no vulgar mind can reach,
No critick thwart, no mighty master teach;
A Charm how mingled of the good and ill!
Yet still so mingled that the mystick whole
Shall captive hold the struggling Gazer's will,
'Till vanquish'd reason own its full control.
And such, oh Rubens, thy mysterious art,
The charm that vexes, yet enslaves the heart!
Thy lawless style, from timid systems free,
Impetuous rolling like a troubled sea,
High o'er the rocks of reason's lofty verge
Impending hangs; yet, ere the foaming surge
Breaks o'er the bound, the refluent ebb of taste
Back from the shore impels the wat'ry waste.

SONNET

To my venerable Friend, the President of the Royal Academy.

FROM one unus'd in pomp of words to raise
A courtly monument of empty praise,
Where self, transpiring through the flimsy pile,
Betrays the builder's ostentatious guile,
Accept, oh West, these unaffected lays,
Which genius claims and grateful justice pays.
Still green in age, thy vig'rous powers impart
The youthful freshness of a blameless heart:
For thine, unaided by another's pain,
The wiles of envy, or the sordid train
Of selfishness, has been the manly race
Of one who felt the purifying grace
Of honest fame; nor found the effort vain
E'en for itself to love thy soul-ennobling art.

THE MAD LOVER

At the Grave of his Mistress.

Stay, gentle Stranger, softly tread!
Oh, trouble not this hallow'd heap.
Vile Envy says my Julia's dead;
But Envy thus will never sleep.

Ye creeping Zephyrs, hist you, pray,
Nor press so hard yon wither'd leaves;
For Julia sleeps beneath this clay—
Nay, feel it, how her bosom heaves!

Oh, she was purer than the stream
 That saw the first created morn ;
Her words were like a sick man's dream
 That nerves with health a heart forlorn.

And who their lot would hapless deem
 Those lovely, speaking lips to view ;
That light between like rays that beam
 Through sister clouds of rosy hue ?

Yet these were to her fairer soul
 But, as yon op'ning clouds on high
To glorious worlds that o'er them roll,
 The portals to a brighter sky.

And shall the glutton worm defile
 This spotless tenement of love,
That like a playful infant's smile
 Seem'd born of purest light above ?

And yet I saw the sable pall
Dark-trailing o'er the broken ground—
The earth did on her coffin fall—
I heard the heavy, hollow sound

Avaunt, thou Fiend! nor tempt my brain
With thoughts of madness brought from
Hell!
No wo like this of all her train
Has Mem'ry in her blackest cell.

'Tis all a tale of fiendish art—
Thou com'st, my love, to prove it so!
I'll press thy hand upon my heart—
It chills me like a hand of snow!

Thine eyes are glaz'd, thy cheeks are pale,
Thy lips are livid, and thy breath
Too truly tells the dreadful tale—
Thou comest from the house of death!

Oh, speak, Beloved! lest I rave;
The fatal truth I'll bravely meet,
And I will follow to the grave,
And wrap me in thy winding sheet.

FIRST LOVE.

*A BALLAD**.

Ah me! how hard the task to bear
The weight of ills we know!
But harder still to dry the tear,
That mourns a nameless wo.

If by the side of Lucy's wheel
I sit to see her spin,
My head around begins to reel,
My heart to beat within.

* This and the two following ballads were written at a very early age, and have already appeared in some of the Periodical Works of their day.

Or when on harvest holliday
　　I lead the dance along,
If Lucy chance to cross my way,
　　So sure she leads me wrong,

If I attempt the pipe to play,
　　And catch my Lucy's eye,
The trembling musick dies away,
　　And melts into a sigh.

Where'er I go, where'er I turn,
　　If Lucy there be found,
I seem to shiver, yet I burn,
　　My head goes swimming round.

I cannot bear to see her smile,
　　Unless she smile on me ;
And if she frown, I sigh the while,
　　But know not whence it be.

Ah, what have I to Lucy done
To cause me so much stir?
From rising to the setting sun
I sigh, and think of her.

In vain I strive to join the throng
In social mirth and ease;
Now lonely woods I stray among,
For only woods can please.

Ah, me! this restless heart I fear
Will never be at rest,
'Till Lucy cease to live, or tear
Her image from my breast.

THE COMPLAINT.

" Oh, had I Colin's winning ease,"
Said Lindor with a sigh,
" So carelessly ordained to please,
I'd every care defy.

" If Colin but for Daphne's hair
A simple garland weave,
He gives it with so sweet an air
He seems a crown to give.

" But, though I cull the fairest flower
That decks the breast of spring,
And posies from the woodland bower
For Daphne's bosom bring,

" When I attempt to give the fair,
With many a speech in store,
My half-form'd words dissolve in air,
I blush and dare no more.

" And shall I then expect a smile
From Daphne on my love,
When every word and look the while
My clownish weakness prove?

" Oft at the close of summer day,
When Daphne wander'd by,
I've left my little flock astray,
And follow'd with a sigh.

" Yet, fearing to approach too near,
I linger'd far behind:
And, lest my step should reach her ear,
I shook at every wind.

" How happy then must Colin be
Who never knew this fear,
Whose sweet address at liberty
Commands the fair-one's ear!

" A smile, a tear, a word, a sigh,
Stand ready at his call;
In me unknown they live and die,
Who have and feel them all."

Ah, simple swain, how little knows
The love-sick mind to scan
Those gifts which real love bestows
To mark the favour'd man.

Secure, let fluent parrots feign
The musick of the dove;
'Tis only in the eye may reign
The eloquence of love.

WILL, THE MANIAC.

A BALLAD.

HARK ! what wild sound is on the breeze ?
'Tis Will, at evening fall
Who sings to yonder waving trees
That shade his prison wall.

Poor Will was once the gayest swain
At village dance was seen ;
No freer heart of wicked stain
E'er tripp'd the moonlight green.

His flock was all his humble pride,
A finer ne'er was shorn;
And only when a lambkin died
Had Will a cause to mourn.

But now poor William's brain is turn'd,
He knows no more his flock;
For when I ask'd "if them he mourn'd,"
He mock'd the village clock.

No, William does not mourn his fold,
Though tenantless and drear;
Some say, a love he never told
Did crush his heart with fear.

And she, 'tis said, for whom he pin'd
Was heiress of the land,
A lovely lady, pure of mind
Of open heart and hand.

And others tell, as *how* he strove
To win the noble fair,
Who, scornful, jeer'd his simple love,
And left him to despair.

Will wander'd then amid the rocks
Through all the live long day,
And oft would creep where bursting shocks
Had rent the earth away.

He lov'd to delve the darksome dell
Where never pierc'd a ray,
There to the wailing night-bird tell,
'How love was turn'd to clay.'

And oft upon yon craggy mount,
Where threat'ning cliffs hang high,
Have I observ'd him stop to count
With fixless stare the sky.

Then to himself, in murmurs low,
Repeating as he wound
Along the mountain's woody brow,
'Till lost was every sound.

But soon he went so wild astray
His kindred ach'd to see ;
And now, secluded from the day,
In yonder cell is he.

W. Pople, Printer, 67, Chancery Lane.

www.ingramcontent.com/pod-product-compliance
Lightning Source LLC
LaVergne TN
LVHW021400110826
845150LV00007B/1723

* 9 7 8 1 4 2 5 5 1 2 8 2 8 *